THE PRIDE OF UNFORGIVENESS

COMPANION

An 8-Day Pathway into Healing, Renewal, and Release

TEMEILA C. DANIEL

CONCISE
PUBLISHING HOUSE

The Pride of Unforgiveness Companion:
An 8-Day Pathway into Healing, Renewal, and Release

ISBN: 979-8-9909626-9-9

Concise Publishing House
120 Preston Executive Drive, Suite 229
Cary, NC 27513
www.ConcisePublishing.us

This Companion Belongs To:

____

Date Begun:

____

This journey is personal.

This work is sacred.

This space is yours.

How to Use This 8-Day Companion Pathway

This companion was not created to replace the book. It was created to **carry the heart work forward**.

The Pride of Unforgiveness confronts the heart. This companion **guides you through the heart work that follows that confrontation**.

Reading exposes.

Heart work transforms.

This is not a devotional.

This is not a journal.

This is a **pathway experience** designed to help you move from awareness into restoration and from understanding into lived freedom.

If You Are Starting Here

If you are holding this companion before reading *The Pride of Unforgiveness*, welcome. This pathway can still serve you. Healing is not limited by order. However, understand this: this companion was designed to **walk alongside the book**, not apart from it.

The book introduces heart exposure. This companion guides heart work.

You may notice moments where reflection feels deeper than explanation. That is intentional. This pathway is built for processing, not teaching. It assumes you have already been invited into the conversation.

If you choose to continue here first, move slowly. Let God meet you where you are, but I strongly encourage you to return to the book when possible. Together, they form a complete healing experience. You will have exposure and restoration working side by side.

You are not behind.

You are simply entering the journey from a different doorway.

Why Eight Days?

In Scripture, the number eight represents **new beginnings, covenant renewal, and spiritual transition**. On the eighth day, covenant identity was established:

"On the eighth day the boy is to be circumcised."
Genesis 17:12 (NLT)

This moment marked more than a physical act. It symbolized **entering a new posture of alignment with God**.

We also see this pattern in the story of Noah:

"Eight people were saved through water."
1 Peter 3:20 (NLT)

After cleansing came renewal.

After judgment came restoration.

After devastation came new beginning.

Eight follows completion and ushers in **transformation beyond the cycle**.

That is why this companion is structured as an **8-Day Pathway**. It is not to revisit pain, but to step fully into healed alignment, restored posture, and forward movement.

How This Pathway Works

Each day invites you into:

- A focused heart theme
- Scripture alignment
- A Prophetic Nudge that directs posture
- Heart Work that brings awareness and honesty
- An Integration Moment that activates application
- Prayer

This is not something you rush through. Some days may feel light. Others may feel tender. Both types of days are part of heart work. This is something you allow to unfold. This is an internal alignment. Healing is not measured by speed. So, move slowly, pause often, and let the truth settle.

The Posture Required for This Journey

You are not being asked to perform healing. You are being invited to **participate in heart work**.

Come on this pathway without defense, without pressure, and without pretending because Heart work requires:

- Willingness
- Honesty
- Surrender
- Stillness

Healing flows freely where humility is present.

Your Eight-Day Commitment

For the next eight days, you are choosing:

- Freedom over familiarity
- Healing over hiding
- Release over residue
- Truth over performance

You are not becoming someone new. You are returning to the version of you that existed before pain reshaped your posture.

Opening Prayer

Father, I enter this pathway with humility and expectation. I open my heart to the work You desire to do within me. Prepare me for honest heart work. Align my spirit with truth and guide me through this journey with grace, clarity, and peace. Lord, I give You permission to work deeper than my words and beyond my understanding. In Jesus' name, Amen.

DAY 1: EXPOSURE

When the heart is invited into truth

Governing Scripture: *Psalm 139:23–24 (NLT)*
"Search me, O God, and know my heart; test me and know my anxious thoughts. Point out anything in me that offends You, and lead me along the path of everlasting life."

Prophetic Nudge

Let truth rise without resistance. What surfaces is not here to overwhelm you; it is opening the door for healing to begin.

Heart Work

What surfaces in the light often reveals what has been carried in silence. God reveals what is hidden because He is ready to heal it. There are places the heart learned to carry quietly, not because you wanted to hold them, but because release was never taught.

You do not need to defend what you feel here. You do not need to explain anything to God. He already knows, and He is present.

Ask Yourself:

- What has God brought to the surface?
- Where have I said "I'm fine" while still carrying weight underneath?
- What has my heart learned to hold in silence?

Integration Moment - Release

Acknowledge what surfaced and bring it before God.

Write it down as an act of surrender, not analysis. Place it in His hands and release what has been hidden into the light of healing.

Prayer

Father, I open my heart to Your truth. I bring before You what has been hidden, guarded, or ignored. I lay down the need to protect what You are ready to heal. Search me with gentleness and lead me into freedom. I trust You with what has surfaced. In Jesus' name, Amen.

Personal Reflection

DAY 2: ROOT REVELATION

When hidden pride is brought into the light

Governing Scripture: *Proverbs 16:18 (KJV)*
"Pride goeth before destruction, and an haughty spirit before a fall."

Prophetic Nudge

God is uncovering what has been shaping your responses beneath the surface. What is revealed is meant to free you, not expose you.

Heart Work

What grows on the surface is rarely the real issue. Bitterness does not grow alone. It is often sustained by roots that remain unseen.

Pride rarely looks like arrogance. Sometimes it looks like composure. Sometimes it looks like independence. Sometimes it looks like silence. It whispers, "I'm fine," and convinces the heart that protection is strength. It tells you distance is wisdom, but pride does not heal, it preserves pain.

God is inviting you to look beneath what has been visible and allow Him to expose what has been quietly shaping your posture. This is not about condemnation. It is about clarity.

Ask yourself:

- Where have I protected myself instead of trusting God?
- What have I called "strength" that may actually be self-preservation?
- Where have I avoided vulnerability to feel safe?

Integration Moment - Renewal

Open the area God has revealed and allow Him to work beneath the surface.

Ask the Lord to uproot what no longer belongs and renew what He desires to restore. Let this become the beginning of deeper healing, not just awareness.

Prayer

Father, I acknowledge the places where pride has lived quietly in my heart. Where self-protection replaced trust and silence felt safer than surrender. I lay down the need to guard what You are ready to heal. Teach me humility where fear once led and restore softness where pain hardened me. In Jesus' name, Amen.

Personal Reflection

____

____

____

____

____

____

____

____

____

DAY 3: REALIGNMENT

When expectation is surrendered and posture is restored

Governing Scripture: *Romans 12:3(NLT)*
"Don't think you are better than you really are. Be honest in your evaluation of yourselves, measuring yourselves by the faith God has given us."

Prophetic Nudge

Expectation has a quiet way of reshaping posture, especially when disappointment goes unexamined. What you have been holding God responsible to deliver may be the very place He is inviting you to release control and return to trust.

Heart Work

Healing eventually reaches the posture of the heart. There is a point in healing where God begins addressing not only what happened to you, but how your heart responded to it.

What started as honest disappointment can slowly shift into expectation. When expectation is left unexamined, it becomes entitlement. Not because the heart is proud, but because pain tried to protect itself.

Grief becomes demand.

Disappointment becomes negotiation.

Trust becomes conditional.

This is where posture shifts. God is not removing your worth. He is restoring alignment.

Ask yourself:

- Where has expectation quietly replaced trust in my heart?
- Have I measured God's goodness by outcomes instead of His presence?
- Where have I compared my process to someone else's timeline?
- What am I still holding God responsible to deliver a certain way?

Integration Moment - Realignment

Identify the expectations you have been carrying quietly.

Bring them before God and ask Him to realign your heart with His will. Release outcomes, timelines, and silent agreements that no longer serve trust.

Prayer

Father, I release every expectation that has replaced trust. I lay down the need to be owed and the timelines I have carried quietly. Restore humility where disappointment hardened my posture. Teach my heart how to trust You again without conditions. In Jesus' name, Amen.

Personal Reflection

____

____

____

____

DAY 4: HONEST SURRENDER

When surface forgiveness gives way to heart release

Governing Scripture: *Matthew 15:8 (NLT)*
"'These people honor me with their lips, but their hearts are far from me."

Prophetic Nudge

When certain memories surface, notice what still tightens in your heart. That tenderness often marks the place where deeper surrender is needed.

Heart Work

Forgiveness can sound complete while healing is still unfinished. There are moments when forgiveness leaves the mouth but has not yet reached the heart.

Words can express forgiveness.

Only surrender releases residue.

It is possible to say "I forgive you" while still guarding emotion. It is possible to move forward while still carrying memory. Healing does not stop where language ends.

Surface forgiveness allows life to continue. Heart surrender allows freedom to settle.

God is not asking you to pretend it didn't happen. He is inviting you to bring what still feels unresolved into His presence.

Ask yourself:

- Where have I said "I forgive you" but still felt emotional weight?
- What memory still tightens something in me when it surfaces?
- Have I avoided addressing pain by calling distance peace?
- What emotion have I released with words but not yet surrendered to God?

Integration Moment - Honest Surrender

Bring what still feels unresolved into God's presence.

Ask the Lord to touch what you have managed instead of surrendered. Allow honesty to lead you into deeper freedom.

Prayer

Father, I bring You what I have tried to cover with words. I admit where I have said I forgave but still carried the weight of memory. I open my heart to honest healing. Touch what still feels tender and heal what I learned to manage instead of surrender. In Jesus' name, Amen.

Personal Reflection

____

____

____

____

____

____

____

____

DAY 5: RELEASE OF CONTROL
When trust replaces fear-based protection

Governing Scripture: *James 4:6–7 (NLT)*
"And he gives grace generously. As the Scriptures say,
"God opposes the proud but gives grace to the humble.""

Prophetic Nudge

Some things have been carried longer than they were meant to be. What you have been holding tightly may be the place God is inviting you to place back in His hands.

Heart Work

Control does not enter loudly. It settles quietly where trust was wounded.

What began as protection slowly becomes posture. That posture begins shaping how you respond, guard, and engage. Control often feels like wisdom. It sounds like **"protecting my peace."** It looks like managing outcomes and rehearsing responses. But what feels like safety can quietly become suffocation.

God never asked you to carry assignments that belong to Him.

He is inviting you to unclench your heart.

Ask yourself:

- Where am I trying to manage outcomes instead of trusting God?
- What situation have I been carrying that was never mine to fix?
- Where has fear disguised itself as responsibility?
- What would it look like to release control and rest in God's leadership?

Integration Moment - Refill

Name the areas where control has lived.

Offer them back to God and ask Him to restore peace where striving has settled. Release what you were never meant to carry and allow trust to refill what fear drained.

Prayer

Father, I release the need to control what You are fully capable of handling. I lay down every outcome I have tried to manage and every situation I have tried to fix. Teach my heart how to trust again. Replace striving with surrender and fear with peace. In Jesus' name, Amen.

Personal Reflection

____

____

____

____

____

____

____

____

DAY 6: STORY REWRITTEN
When God reclaims authorship
over your narrative

Governing Scripture: *Romans 8:28 (NLT)*
"And we know that God causes everything to work together for the good of those who love God and are called according to his purpose for them."

Prophetic Nudge

The narrative you have been living from matters. What you have carried as truth may need to be placed back in God's hands so He can restore meaning.

Heart Work

Pain tries to define your identity. It assigns labels. It reshapes how you see yourself and how you interpret your past.

Rejected.

Overlooked.

Betrayed.

Forgotten.

Pain is not your author. God does not erase what happened. He redeems its meaning. He does not remove the memory. He removes its authority. What once wounded you no longer has permission to narrate who you are becoming.

Healing begins when the heart releases old interpretations and allows God to reframe the story through truth instead of trauma.

Ask yourself:

- What part of my story have I allowed pain to define?
- Where have I attached meaning that God is asking me to release?
- What label have I carried that no longer belongs to me?
- What would it look like to trust God with the narrative of this season?

Integration Moment - Reposition

Bring your story before God again.

Ask Him to reframe what you misunderstood and restore meaning where pain has spoken. Release old interpretations and allow redemption to reshape perspective.

Prayer

Father, I release the story I have been telling myself. I lay down every label that pain tried to place on me. I surrender every interpretation that no longer aligns with Your truth. Reclaim authorship over my life and rewrite what hurt tried to define. In Jesus' name, Amen.

Personal Reflection

____

____

____

____

DAY 7: RESTORED RHYTHM

When the heart learns to move in grace again

Governing Scripture: *Matthew 11:28–30 (MSG)*
"Are you tired? Worn out? Burned out on religion? Come to me. Get away with me and you'll recover your life. I'll show you how to take a real rest. Walk with me and work with me—watch how I do it. Learn the unforced rhythms of grace. I won't lay anything heavy or ill-fitting on you. Keep company with me and you'll learn to live freely and lightly."

Prophetic Nudge

Pressure has been leading long enough. God is inviting grace to take the lead again in how you move, respond, and carry responsibility.

Heart Work

When life becomes heavy, it is often because the heart has slipped out of rhythm with grace. Grace carries a rhythm. Heaven moves with a pace.

When life becomes heavy, it is often because the heart has slipped out of alignment with God's cadence. Responsibility grows loud. Pressure becomes normal. Movement continues, but peace fades.

Jesus never called you to perform healing. He called you to walk with Him.

Stillness is not inactivity.

It is alignment.

Rest is not escape.

It is restoration.

Healing does not end when pain lifts. It matures when the heart learns how to live differently. This is the invitation to stop running ahead of God and begin moving with Him again.

Ask yourself:

- Where have I been moving faster than grace was meant to carry me?

- Have I confused productivity with purpose?

- What part of my life feels rushed instead of rested?

- What would it look like to walk with God instead of running ahead of Him?

Integration Moment - Resettling

Offer your pace to God.

Ask Him to restore rhythm and teach your heart how to remain with Him.

Let grace reset how you move, respond, and carry responsibility.

Prayer

Father, I release every pace that never came from You. I lay down hurry, pressure, and striving. Teach my heart how to walk with You again. Restore rhythm where life became heavy and replace exhaustion with grace. In Jesus' name, Amen.

Personal Reflection

DAY 8: DISCERNMENT RESTORED

When spiritual clarity is protected and the heart is guarded from distortion

Governing Scripture: *Proverbs 4:23 (NLT)*
"Guard your heart above all else, for it determines the course of your life."

Prophetic Nudge

What has been healed now needs to be guarded. Stay aware of subtle shifts in thought and posture that try to pull the heart back into old patterns.

Heart Work

Freedom requires stewardship. Healing brings restoration, but restoration must be guarded.

Not every voice that sounds wise is aligned with truth. Not every familiar thought deserves agreement. After deliverance, the greatest threat is not always obvious temptation, it is subtle distortion.

This is what twists perception:

Old patterns trying to resurface. Former mindsets attempting to regain influence. Emotional reactions disguised as discernment.

The heart must now learn how to guard what God has restored without becoming defensive or hardened. Discernment is not suspicion. It is clarity rooted in truth and humility.

What God has healed in you must now be protected through awareness, obedience, and alignment.

Ask yourself:

- Where do I need to guard my heart more intentionally?
- What thought patterns have tried to return that no longer belong to me?
- Have I confused emotional reaction with spiritual discernment?
- What helps me stay anchored in truth and not drift back into old thinking?

Integration Moment - Guarding Clarity

Bring your heart posture before God.

Ask Him to strengthen discernment and keep you aligned with truth. Choose to guard what He has restored by remaining responsive to His leading.

Prayer

Father, thank You for restoring my heart and renewing my mind. Help me guard what You have healed and remain aligned with Your truth. Sharpen my discernment and protect me from distortion, distraction, and old patterns trying to return. Keep my heart anchored in You. In Jesus' name, Amen.

Personal Reflection

____

____

____

____

____

Sealed in Alignment

Alignment is sealed when truth, posture, and surrender come into agreement with God, not by effort but by grace.

You have not simply completed eight days.

You have shifted posture.

What was exposed has been surrendered.

What was rooted has been uprooted.

What was heavy has been released.

What was fractured has been realigned.

This is not the end of the work.

It is the beginning of a new way of living.

Healing is not something you visit.

It is something you carry.

You now move forward with:

Greater awareness

Deeper humility

Stronger discernment

Restored rhythm

And guarded clarity

Do not rush to explain what changed.

Let your life reveal it.

Walk gently.

Stay aware.

Remain aligned.

What God healed in you is not fragile.

It is fortified by truth.

This work is now sealed in alignment.

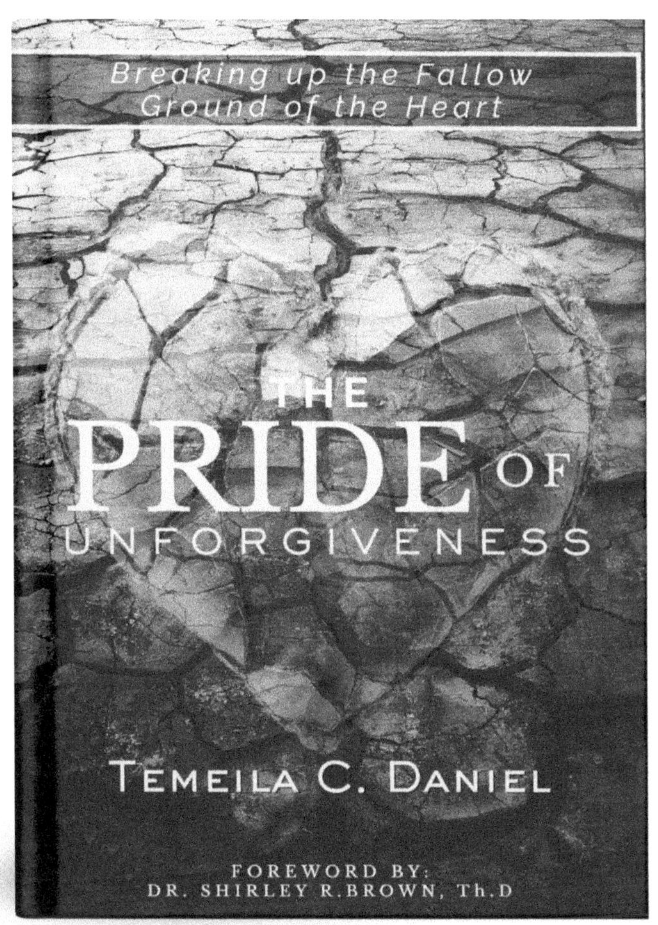

The Pride of Unforgiveness: Breaking Up the Fallow Ground of the Heart introduces the heart exposure that begins this journey.

The Pride of Unforgiveness Companion: An 8-Day Pathway into Healing, Renewal, and Release was created to walk alongside the book and carry the heart work forward.

ALSO BY
TEMEILA C. DANIEL

A Guide to Virtual
Meeting

Chaos to Organization
40 Day Journal

A Tool to Understanding and
Interpreting Your Dreams

CONTINUE THE JOURNEY

ELDER TEMEILA C. DANIEL

- TEACHING & MASTERCLASSES
- LEADERSHIP WORSKSHOPS
- CHURCH & EVENT SPEAKING

CONNECT WITH ME

Where the Kingdom and the Marketplace Meet

TemeilaDaniel.com

CONCISE
PUBLISHING HOUSE

This work was stewarded under the Concise Publishing House imprint, a curated house committed to bringing purpose-driven manuscripts to publication with clarity, integrity, and care.

Publishing & Production
Book Design & Formatting
ISBN & Distribution Guidance
Author Support

www.ConcisePublishing.us

The Sustainable Transformation Pathway

The *Sustainable Transformation Pathway* is designed to produce lasting transformation for the reader while creating sustainable *authority, impact, and stewardship* for the author.

This pathway centers the reader's experience, guiding them beyond *information* into *integration*. It is *not built for momentary inspiration,* but for *measurable change* — *encouraging reflection, application, and forward movement that extends beyond the final page.*

When a work is aligned with the *Sustainable Transformation Pathway*, it is intentionally structured to *support growth that is lived, not just learned.*

www.ingramcontent.com/pod-product-compliance
Lightning Source LLC
Chambersburg PA
CBHW040112150726
48005CB00013B/1673